MY
ABSOLUTE
HEART

MY
ABSOLUTE
HEART

RYAN SAM TURNER

First published in 2022
by Balladeer Books Limited

Printed and bound by CPI Group (UK) Ltd, Croydon, CR0 4YY

A CIP record for this book is available from the British Library.

ISBN: 978-0-9562570-5-5

for her

contents

this beautiful world

If the beautiful things in the world got lost
where would we be?
In some fictitious landscape
surrounded by people and trees.
A smile from a face would be lost,
gone, without a trace.
Joy is missed
like a first kiss,
or a summer's day.
And the only things left in the air
are anger, depression ... and despair.

as you walk through the door

I couldn't sleep the night before –
nerves overwhelming me.
So worried about *what to say* –
or worse – any awkward silences.

The thought of cancelling
was always there.
But I think I already knew …
there was something *special* about you.

I get to the bar early –
for a few nerve-numbing drinks.
And as you walk through the door,
I have already fallen in love.

Those eyes of yours – pulling me in.
Your teeth – gleaming.
Everything about you, makes me forget
… my own insecurities.

Greeting each other with a kiss on the cheek,
I breathe in – you smell so sweet.

mountains

Her cheeks are delicately moulded –
curving her face, blushed red and warm.
They're mountain contours I desperately want to scale,
to kiss and touch and lick
and slide back down.

Gallant lips: plump and inviting
on a girl so nervous, who is visibly quaking.
When she speaks,
she has an innocent tone,
a mellifluous voice that comforts my fall.

lips

Our second date – I was even more nervous,
and no alcohol *today* to steady myself.

But even with only coffee and hot chocolate,
we still chatted like we were already intimate.

I went to order a couple more drinks,
and spotted something to make you smile.

We were just talking about them: Tunnock's Teacakes –
this had to be fate deciding to help me out.

I brought one back, setting it on the table –
an expression of joy crossed your face.

You unwrapped it, tried to eat it elegantly,
an impossible task, most would agree.

But I really loved seeing you like that,
natural and messy, happy with me.

The sticky mallow clinging to your lips,
daft and endearing, sweeter than sweet.

we kiss

we kiss with tongues
our eyes shut tight
this is the moment i've wanted
all of my life

not the best setting – the bar, outside the toilets –
but i've waited too long and the time was never right

i pull you in close and take the plunge –
you let me in – our mouths are one

tuning out the world – the way it should be –
the only two people alive are you and me

we break away and i feel your breath,
warm and moist – a gentle mist, filming my face

you had me then, with that first kiss –
taking my life, which i was happy to give

fireworks

i could be the fire
i could be the flame
i could conquer your imagination
lose myself in your brain
we could be lovers
for more than one night
we could start fireworks
we could bring the light

electricity

I hold your hand
as onstage the band begins –
a song we will come to know so well.

In the middle of the room
surrounded by strangers
it feels like only *we* exist.

I can feel it happening,
in my throat,
in my chest –
love.

My heart beats hard,
and my legs go weak –
I can feel the electricity.

It flows through you
to me –
and back again.

Synapses are snapping,
I can't catch my breath.
I am so happy.

the operation

As routine as it was,
fear consumed my every thought.
Not the fear of dying,
but the fear of being without you.
Not to see your face
or hear your voice –
that was the most terrifying thing.

I put my belongings
in a plastic bag,
and send my final messages –
it is nearly time to go.

I sit in the waiting room,
in my robe,
the television on,
a lump lodged in my throat.

My name is called,
my fate imminent.
I can feel my heart pounding
against its cage of bone.

The general anaesthetic is injected
and I wait for the drugs to take me away.
I fight and hold on for as long as I can,
making sure I am thinking of you.

palmistry

We compared scars. I showed her the evidence of my operation –
the distressed trail on the inside of my wrist. I invited her to
touch it, to feel the hardened line of healed skin. She didn't
flinch at my request but ran her index finger slowly along the
silvery-white track.

I shivered all over, my whole body charged with electricity.

The hairs on my arms bristled, the skin beneath covered in
goose pimples. I'm sure she witnessed this – but she didn't say
anything, sparing my blushes.

She showed me a tiny scar on the underside of her hand.
Hardly noticeable, blending in with the palm lines that almost
camouflaged it.

I think she wanted me to touch her as well.

Feigning interest in her playground mishap, I held her hand
in mine, looking into her eyes as I caressed the damage. She
shivered too. I didn't mention it.

candle

we go to the brewery bar
and play those silly card games,
laughing so hard
that we can barely speak

drinking and smiling,
we are so relaxed,
sitting opposite you –
i know i'm in love

the night turns late
and a candle is placed
on our table,
lighting your glowing face

the flame flickers
and tickles your chin,
your cheeks are gilded –
i know i'm in love

afternoon sessions and romantic nights

i felt the same way every single time –
the irregular heartbeat that told me i was alive

hot breath kisses
tongues entwined
saliva on my chin
yours mixed with mine

the impulsive sessions in the afternoon –
through the front door, straight to the bedroom

biting lips
stroking thighs
we are both shaking
as i enter inside

or the romantically planned nights –
music, scented candles, foreplay, dimmed lights

it always ended too quickly
– i'm sorry about that
i just loved you so much
it was never an act

two little stars

It was our first time of actually *sleeping* together –
the part that was more intimate to me.

Holding one another under the billowing sheets –
our legs tangled, entwined, barriers breached.

Heads resting on the fluffy pillows –
we swapped stories of our lives before.

The light turned off, we shared a *goodnight* kiss –
I took one last look in your eyes before I shut mine.

Two little stars, glittering in your darkened room –
a memory to brighten the bleakest of nights.

topography

Under the cold sheets
hot-water bottles keep us warm.
We are cocooned together;
I can feel your heat.
My hands move around
your faultless form,
while my mind scans and traces
the topography of your perfection.

the crawler

her crooked fingers crawl
over my skin
making their way
up my backbone
climbing the stairs
of my animate skeleton

her finger-steps tickle
like strokes from a feather
i squirm and curl
then tense
'til i'm still

the waiting is over …
i'm blooming –
let me unfurl

not the best lover

Jet-black curtains in her bedroom
blanket out the jealous moon.
Her bed sheets are spotless, white and fresh.
Sliding beneath, we take equal deep breaths.
Here we are, in this strange, awkward moment.
Moves are made and I'm shaking with intent.
In the darkness our tongues entwine;
our tattoos touch, hers kissing mine.
All of a sudden, the moment is over.
To be truthful, I'm not the best lover.
Laughing it off, she tells me to forget it.
We are in love: in the morning I can prove it.

moths

the moths are attracted
to your eyes,
big and bright
like lamps
or stars,
celestially glowing,
drawing them in
with your orange-blue stare.

spoon

My chest pressed against her back –
she can feel the beating of my heart.

Our bare legs, hinged and twisted –
knees bent, we're interlocked.

My cold hands wrap around her belly –
she shakes and spasms as my fingers glide.

I kiss her shoulder and say 'goodnight',
and we spoon together through the night.

weightless in my arms

We walk down the tiled stairs,
into the chilled water of the pool.
Splashing one another,
our bodies quickly turn warm.
Swimming lengths side by side,
a race I never want to end.
You twine yourself around me
and you are weightless in my arms.
We exchange chlorine kisses,
but I can still taste *you* on my lips.

flesh on flesh

To be naked with someone, bare flesh on flesh, brings so much emotion. To feel their dimpled skin shiver to your touch, to feel the beat of their heart flutter and stumble, to hear the rhythm of their voice tremble – these are things no drug can replicate.

personal sun

We sit in the shadow of Arthur's Seat –
an extinct volcano – our city's peak.
We're both slightly hungover and feeling spent.
What are Sundays actually for, after all?
Sprawled out on your leopard-print blanket,
we gorge on a fast-food takeaway.
The jackets we brought are not required,
so they are rolled into pillows for our fuzzy heads.
Flat on our backs, orange rays beam down on us
as our fingers dance over each other's skin.
The smell of the grass and your sweet perfume,
brings a headiness that I've never known.
After a while, we just lie, not moving,
arms and legs twined lovingly.
We are two individuals trying to be one –
lovers under our personal sun.
My heated blood travels through my body,
I can feel my face turning scarlet red.
If I died right now, holding your hand,
I don't think there could be a happier man.

slow dance

It's a Saturday night and we're on the couch –
another summer's evening slipping away.

Then …

You lean over and kiss my mouth,
your lips cool against my fever heat.

I put some music on, then take your hand.

We slow dance in the living room to *our* song,
spurred on by one too many pink gins.

This is what I've always wanted.

Holding each other as tight as can be,
we sway seductively from side to side.

You say:
'No one's ever danced with me like this before.'

I'm glad that I gave you that.

boulders

Bounding through the woods,
your hand in mine,
our feet move quickly
over the parched land.
Our steps snap sticks,
crunch through leaves.
A soft, warm wind
brings a subtle relief.
We make it to the rocks,
the boulders as old as time,
where we'll sit and love,
as constant as stone.

fortress

We walk along the city's main thoroughfare –
the shops of my youth no longer there.

Once fancy stores with classical names,
are now full of tat and touristy things.

But Princes Street's still busy with manic shoppers,
when all we want to do is stroll leisurely around.

So, we cross the road, escaping to the gardens,
and find a spot on the vastly occupied grass.

Your eyes are locked, in wonder on the castle,
as it bulges and muscles out of the sedimentary rock.

I wrap my arms protectively around you – we combine –
creating our own impregnable fortress.

everything i want, everything i need

you are the butterflies in my gut
the dryness in my mouth
you are the tremors in my legs
the killer of my doubts

you are the swirling in my head
the sweat beads on my skin
you are the trembling of my voice
my confidence within

you are the beating of my heart
the beauty in my dreams
you are everything i want
you are everything i need

the greatest tide

We leave the busy foreshore,
crossing the causeway to the tidal island.
The path is protected by concrete pylons –
reminders of its violent past.
Sharing the tarmac with intrigued tourists,
I pull you close when the walkway narrows.

If anyone is going to fall, it will be me.

The island is covered in bright green grass –
seagulls squawking and gliding overhead.
Making our way up the sandy hill,
we enter a graffitied fortification.
I stare out of the ruin's window,
watching the sea with you by my side.

The water is rising, better keep an eye on the time.

Sitting for a while, in comfortable silence,
we pop the heads off daisies as people leave.
The sea is beginning to crash and warn,
swallowing more of the land we're on.
We wait until the very last second,
and for a moment – the island is our very own.

We walk quickly, back across the vanishing stone.

We make it – barely – with just seconds to spare –
drawing panicked breaths of the salty air.
Back on regular terra firma,
we have left our idyll behind –
just you and me on the island,
surrounded by the greatest tide.

explosions

The sun is setting as we leave the flat,
searching for a vantage point.
We make our way to Calton Hill,
bundling quickly up the concrete steps.

The summit is the strangest sight:
a monument unfinished since 1829,
surrounded by tourists, families, lovers …
teenagers guzzling tonic wine.

We find a space, but it's not ideal:
constantly being barged by drunks,
the people in front far too tall –
not the romantic setting I'd hoped for.

So, we quickly abandon that location,
looking for somewhere a little more relaxed.
But none exist; everyone's got the same idea,
and the fireworks are about to begin.

In the end, we have to watch them from the street.

The rockets fly, whistle, and bang,
kaleidoscopic colours illuminate the sky.
She stands there still, silent, mesmerised,
while I watch the explosions in her eyes …

because that's all that I want to see.

like ghosts do

Be still, your breath.
In the winter chill
your exhalations float
… like ghosts
and vanish
… like ghosts.
Evaporate.
Be still, be still,
be still, your breath.

neon lights and noises

we walk along the promenade –
the glacial sea breeze setting us free

our frozen hands linked together –
with you is the warmest place to be

we pause to watch the cold-water swimmers –
laughing at their misplaced bravery

then stop by a quaint little café –
where the heat inside is heavenly

we go to the archaic amusements –
childhood memories come suddenly

overwhelmed by people, neon lights and noises –
it still feels like it's only *you* and *me*

(vegan) afternoon tea

It was the third of December – your birthday –
and I had it all planned out perfectly.
Make love in the morning, open your presents –
get showered, changed, visit your parents.

Go tenpin bowling with lots of laughter,
waste some money at the swindling arcades.
Back home, recuperate, get clothed in finery,
wait for a taxi to take us on our way.

As we travelled to your main surprise,
I could see the excited gleam in your eyes.
Arriving at our city's grandest hotel –
adorned exquisitely in festive lights.

We had our (vegan) afternoon tea,
in the shadow of a colossal Christmas tree.
And then we sipped warm mulled wine
as the dark night outside pressed in.

With our bellies full, we crawled through our regular bars –
places that were once *mine*, *yours*, but were now *ours*,
ending at the place where we first met.
Now I wish I could have that time again.

I hope I made you feel *special* on your *special* day –
and this year was going to be even more so …
I was going to ask a question, which I hoped,
would make an honest woman out of you …

and the happiest man alive out of me.

marshmallow

We walk around the Royal Botanic Garden –
the trees and plants covered in Christmas lights.

We're warm beneath our hats and scarves –
but our frost-bitten noses don't feel like they're ours.

Hot drinks are cupped to relieve the freeze –
and together we amble through the frosted leaves.

Stopping at the overpriced marshmallow stall,
we choose some flavours I would never imagine at all.

We toast them on the fire, which was purposely built,
to add more romance to this loving night.

The melted mallow sticks to your lips,
and you give me the best sweet-sticky kiss.

midnight mass

We sit on the stiff wooden pews,
my hand resting on your shivering thigh,
and yours on mine.

Singing from the dusty hymnals,
a thing I never thought I'd do.
But I am here with you.

The reverend preaches to his congregation,
reciting Nativity stories
that hold us enraptured.

The bell chimes for midnight,
I bow my head
and pray to my new God.

I pray for every Christmas to be like this …
me sitting here with you.

panic attack

i knew it was over
months in advance
the day i called you
having *that* panic attack

'i'm going to lose everything …
i'm going to lose you!'

you disagreed with me
… but it still came true

statistic

The festivities have ended.
The excitement is gone.
It's just a standard dark morning –
feeling lost and alone.

I drive away from your flat,
knowing that things are wrong.
Your lack of any *goodbye*,
no words, nothing, says it all …

Hoping for a distraction,
I turn the radio on.
People discuss *January*,
the *break-up* month.

Percentages, reasons and rationale
a new year, a fresh start … without me.
I change the station as fast as I can,
but our ending now feels inevitable.

Only a few days before,
I was told I was loved –
that you were happy with me
and how I was dealing with my anxiety.

Just a short time later
we've become another statistic.
And I really thought …
we were more than that.

bees

My body is a nest of friction –
a swarm of bees buzzing through me.

Every hair on it is upstanding –
with fizzing, bristling anxiety.

I lie in bed with my weak jaw clenched –
teeth grinding until the enamel erodes.

My brain motors, I cannot focus –
only a spiral of lost ideas and thoughts.

If I could just relax, and release –
I could become the man I long to be.

pyrotechnics

fireworks are going off inside my head –
jarring explosive thoughts
(whistle → BANG!)
that want me dead

pressure builds and the rockets explode –
a cascade of dazzling lights confusing me

the whooshing, crackling sounds fill me with fear –
all i want is for my brain to be clear

sulphur-smoke ghosts spiral up my nose –
besieging what was left of my rational self

i pray and beg for this display to end –
is it too much to ask …
to feel calm and normal again?

silvering

i stand outside your building,
staring up at your second-floor window –
the light is on – i know you're home

pressing your buzzer – i wait,
my heart beating hard as i hope for an answer –
no acknowledgement comes

all i wanted to do was *talk*
and make everything *right* –
the wrong thing to do – in hindsight

stepping back, i look again at your glass
a rectangle of blackness now –
i know in that moment what your decision is

i am left on the pavement, on your street,
a full moon shining down on me,
silvering my stream of tears

one single tear

I didn't even receive a call – no spoken words at all –
only a carefully phrased message sent to my phone.
Surely I was worth more than that?

My belongings dropped off at my workplace,
left with my confused colleagues and friends.
Surely I was worth more than that?

I had to beg for one last face-to-face.
We sat in your car where I cried and cried.
But to you I wasn't worth one single tear.

two bags that broke my heart

they were waiting for me
like bullies at the back gates
after school

the sight of them made me shiver
and splutter for breath
all too final – all too real

my heart and head pulverised
by seeing my belongings
crammed into two bags

i've stored them in my car
unable to accept
i've ruined my life
once again

the conversation in the car

Your reply was immediate:
melancholic, angry;
your mood reflected
in your eyes.
Their blank stare,
the numbness that I've caused.
The love I suffocated in you.

Shivers race up my spine –
the ineffable horror of my loss
sinks its claws deep
into the nape of my neck
and settles there.

It is stomach-turning; sickening.
My rivulet of tears
turns into a flood.
Guttural screams ring
through my mind.

Nimbus clouds are forming,
the sky turning black.
The light inside the car fades,
and the rain begins to tap,
and then beat, on the roof.

I beg, plead, for another chance –
but it's all too late.
They were too serious –
the mistakes that I made.   »

My face changes shape,
struggling to contain the tears.
My heart is broken,
I am empty inside.

The realisation hits me hard –
this is the last time I'll ever see you.
Totally desolate, I leave the car.
My self-destructive ways have won again.

Now I must try and live
with only my interminable regret.

flat battery

You're staring back at me
in the rear-view mirror.
Standing here –
I barely feel like a man.

Words are exchanged between us
but nothing's about to change.
Our parting of ways over,
you start the car.

Eyes fail to meet,
the closeness is gone.
You drive away without looking back,
trailing engine fumes in your wake.

Swirling around, they try to choke me,
suffocate me, overwhelm me.
Gusts of wind disperse them –
my bone-chilling saviour.

Your car is just a memory,
a scene played out in the past,
and I am left standing in the road
… my battery flat.

out of focus

The photograph is blurred and fuzzy
but it remains my everlasting image of us.

We stand at the bottom of some marble stairs,
doubled over and laughing hard.

Our faces are just waves of colour
but I can still make out expressions of delight.

The one thing that is absolutely clear
is the way we felt about each other then.

lambent light

When I eventually drift off to sleep –
the world is condensed into a pool of darkness.

The infinite blackness that fills my dreams,
appears to travel on and on and on.

Then … when I least expect it … light appears:
a lambent strobe from your flickering eyes.

You stare at me as I stare at you …
and I never want to wake again.

in static

You were in my dreams last night,
but even there
you were a ghost,
a faceless presence.
Your voice crackled,
almost drowned in static.
'Help me,' you said.
'I just want to be free.'

So do I.

kaleidoscope: part one

It started with colours only. The blackness of my sleep interrupted by bolts of crimson – a deep-red lightning storm overpowering my dormant brain. Other colours quickly introduced themselves. Ice-blue beams shot through the red flashes, creating an offshoot of magenta. Drops of purple rain fell from the chaos. Blazing yellow arrows darted all over, leaving trails of gold in their wake. Emerald green spreads around the periphery. Then the rest of the rainbow arrived and a theatrical dance of colour waltzed before me, illuminating the twilight. And then she came.

jigsaw

put me together –
piece by piece

all my interlocking parts –
carefully slotted in place

how you loved solving things –
never accepting defeat

until i became ... the only puzzle
you ever chose to abandon

more than a memory

Eventually, I will stop messaging.
One day will turn into two,
two into three, and so on.

You will be reduced to just a memory,
a part of my past,
a fleeting thought throughout the day.

Please don't let things end this way –
you should be more than just a memory to me.

oh, the love i feel

The first time that I saw *those* eyes
I knew I'd be mesmerised
by their mystic marble of green-brown.
The sweet smell of your perfume
that you thought was overbearing
was anything but to me.
Oh, the love I feel.

You made me watch TV shows
that I never normally would,
but I didn't mind ... not with you.
I'd just sit there, sneaking glimpses of your face,
and smile to myself,
marvelling at how lucky I was.
Oh, the love I feel.

Lying on the couch
our bodies intertwined
I'd play with the toes
of your tiny feet,
twisting them in ways
that made you shiver and squeal.
Oh, the love I feel.

Listening to the bands playing,
I stand behind you,
my arms wrapped lovingly around.
My chin on your shoulder,
we are cheek to cheek,
my stubbled jaw touching your pearlescent skin.
Oh, the love I feel.   »

48

Tucked up in bed with you,
I'd wait for the funny way we'd say
those three special words
every night without fail,
then a kiss on your lips
and I would sleep so well.
Oh, the love I feel.

Please can we play pinball again
in one of the bars
that we used to frequent?
I still go to them … alone,
and smile at the empty chair opposite,
pretending you have never gone.
Oh, the love I feel.

I could list all the romantic clichés
that I still believe are true:
you are perfect for me,
I am perfect for you.
I want to give you everything,
I want to marry you.
Oh, the love I feel.

The tumultuous way that it all unravelled –
I will never forgive myself.
All my caterwauling,
and the desperate, despicable acts
that I thought would win you back,
are traits I wish I'd never shown.
Oh, how sorry I am.   »

It all ended in ways so wrong,
but my brain was melted ... gone,
not allowing me to be the man I *really* am.
You know me, {Insert Name Here},
and all the good things I gave you,
I want to give again.
Oh, the love I feel.

Everyone will tell you
not to try again,
their scepticism understandable,
but I would prove them all wrong.
I want to *take care* of you,
the way you took care of me.
Oh, the love I feel.

Oh, the love I feel for you –
{Insert Name Here} –
is too much, too special, too true.
I will always have love for you.

Oh, the love I feel.
Oh, the love I feel.

crystalline failures

All the tears I've cried
have left crystalline streaks
staining my cheeks.

In the mirror I see
– the shiny trails
– the tracks of my mistakes
that map my failures with you.

I am so sorry.

constrictor

'i don't love you anymore'

slither ...
her words coil around me
squeeze ...
until i cannot breathe

my bones are breaking
with splintering sounds
my organs bursting
with audible *pops!*

she shuts off my blood –
the oxygen i need
my weak heart stutters
with failing beats

i am now a skeleton sack –
the softest of shells
and that is when ...
she swallows me whole

the bracelet

The bracelet that she bought me,
with our own special inscription,
I now need to take off
or it will serve as a constant reminder
of the greatest love I ever lost.

But I already know
that my bracelet-bare wrist
will not feel right at all.

fragments

I hope there are fragments of me
still in your mind.

I hope you see flashes of us
from time to time.

I hope there are fragments of you
that still think kindly of me.

indelible

She can delete all photographic evidence
– the record of my time with her –
that's completely her choice.
But I was still there. It all still happened.

I will live on in her memories, as she does in mine.
I may be forgotten for a while, but not forever.
The mark she left on me is indelible;
I know the same is true of my mark on her.

bookmark

I still use a photo of you
as a bookmark –
a stupid thing to do.

Before bed, every night,
I read – and see your face
marking my page.

And then I wonder why I cannot sleep ...
such a stupid thing to do.

perfume

Opening notes of pink peppercorn, pear and ruby red grapefruit, and then the heart of it – juicy fuchsia peony with hints of vanilla. It was refreshing … sweet and sexy. This would become her signature scent.

It's funny how you get used to a particular fragrance being a part of your life – an aroma that accompanies your living hours. I was sure I would experience her bouquet for the rest of my days.

But … now … it's gone. And as each monotonous day goes by, my memory of her redolence evaporates a little more. Occasionally, I will experience vague hints of it as I wander through life – and will think she's nearby.

She never is.

all those pretty words

what happened …
to all those pretty words
– that you spoke
– that you wrote

when i'm feeling strong enough
i revisit your letters –
the ones declaring your love
for me … forever

i can imagine your voice
reading them aloud –
all those beautiful promises
that are torture to me now

when we were we

i contemplate leaving this city
escaping the scenes
where we once flourished

the possibility of seeing her
at one of *our* locations
is a thought i just cannot bear

the streets we walked are tainted –
full of everlasting memories
of what might have been

every corner that i turn
i'm met with another reminder
of you and me when we were we

would leaving this city really set me free?

given more

i wish i could have given you more
given more than just myself

more than just my played-out body
more than just my clouded mind
more than our petty arguments
more than my rancid jealousy

i wish i could have given you more

apparitions

As the car pulls into the driveway
the grand, Gothic castle comes into view.

Two turrets bulge like shoulder blades,
hunching up from its gabled roof.

It is still medieval, but much has changed:
a hotel now, hosting weddings … and *us*.

Once we're inside, it is eerily quiet –
the creaking floorboards echo, *and echo … and …*

Up the spiral stairs to our room –
the door shuts itself behind us and we're alone.

Collapsing on the bed, we stare upward –
we've never seen a ceiling so high.

We swap stories about *genuine* sightings –
the ghosts that are meant to haunt this place.

Staring out of the dormer windows,
we envisage the violence that has happened here.

Then we take a walk, swim, drink and eat –
make love at night and then repeat.

Our break away together passes far too quickly –
I could live that time for the rest of my life.

During our stay, I didn't witness any apparitions,
but now I am haunted by these echoes of you.

patience

you gave up on me
at the peak of my anxiety

i was doing all that i could
trying to push myself through

and all that i needed
was a little patience from you

the fall

You were aware of my symptoms –
the surroundings that caused me to panic.
But still you made plans without consultation –
setting me up for an emotional tumble.

Made to feel guilty when I couldn't function,
and made to feel guilty when I tried and failed.
When I thought I'd achieved a significant goal,
I was consistently told that I had not.

I went jogging nearly every morning,
through the pitch-black, frosted, empty streets.
I read self-help books, drank special teas –
even switched to decaffeinated coffee!

Breathing exercises, meditation,
mindfulness and medication.
Some weird tapping therapy –
which I never want to do again.

I was still loving to you, right to the very end.
Remember the rose in your letterbox
and how that made you smile then?
But what did I get in return?

It took time for the pills to settle, to work.
Was that even taken into account?
Sometimes I think that it was all on purpose …
giving you a way out, letting me take the fall.

disintegrate

you said that you'd never leave me
you said that you wanted to be my wife

i would never have left you
i wanted you for all my life

i suffered a passing illness i couldn't control,
you showed barely any compassion at all
it was a difficult spell, i admit –
but where was the encouragement?

if the roles were reversed and i were you,
i would have done everything …
NO! I WOULD HAVE DONE ANYTHING …
to help you see it through

just a few months of pain
was all that was in the way
of a life full of love and happy days –
but *you* let all of that disintegrate

the last package

i send one last package to your flat,
containing trinkets and letters
from our past –
and i wait and i hope …

that these souvenirs will trigger something,
which may bring back to you –
all the reasons why we fell in love
and i hope and i wait …

accoutrements of you

what will i do
with all the accoutrements of you?

they're still in a bag
monopolising my floor
and me
all these months on

when i'm feeling bad
i put my head in close
taking the deepest breath
inhaling the last of you

the biggest mistake

I woke up in a fit of panic,
finally knowing, realising,
that you were gone.
It had taken far too long.

My head spun,
swirled and spiralled,
with kaleidoscopic
visions of you.
Goaded by alcohol,
it was total delirium.

I cried, and gasped,
and feared for myself.
I needed to hear your voice,
one last time.
And that's when I acted out
the biggest mistake of my life.

toxic hands

Puncture my skin
and crack me open –
rib by rib.

Remove what is good,
the best parts of me,
and hide them wisely
safe from my disease.

Ensure I'll never find them
… and poison them
with my toxic hands.

excavation games

Excavate your way
to the centre of my heart.

Crawl through the rubble,
the dirt,
the dust,
past all the slimy insects
that inhabit my body.

Be wary of my mouth,
my beguiling words,
for they seem to slip out
and strangulate
even the hardest
(of women).

My bones – fossils now –
will educate,
revealing stories,
divulging secrets
and admitting to failures
that in life
were too shameful to concede.

Swim through my blood,
keeping your head raised;
use a fast front crawl
to avoid being sucked in
by the swirling current
of my dishonesty.   »

There's an abscess swelling
on the surface of my gut.
Walk tentatively,
making sure not to burst it
and allow the poison to spill out
and ruin it all.

And if … if you locate my heart,
please bring it back to being,
but be prepared to accept
my finite displays
of emotion
and interest.

there was a time ...

There was a time in my life
when you didn't exist.
I had never seen your face,
held your hand, kissed your lips.

Then we became lovers
and everything changed.
I could never imagine
my life without you again.

But here it is;
we are strangers once more –
this haunts me, taunts me,
sickens me to my core.

beautiful claws

Love – the most overpowering emotion. It has the ability to seize your heart. To stop it dead. It puts its beautiful claws around you and squeezes magnificently – and you are filled with a happiness, a sense of purpose, greater than you could ever have imagined. Then its grasp becomes too tight. It starts to constrain you, to warp you, into a mangled, distorted version of yourself.

I look back to the time when she was a stranger to me, and after that our meeting and falling in love. For a while it felt stronger than life itself. But now love has loosened its claws. Free again, we are left with memories – of good times and regrets.

pistanthrophobia

Bad things had happened in your past,
mistakes made by another man.
The things he did, the things he said –
I never did receive the entire tale.
But you gave him chances
that you never gave me.
You had already decided
what our outcome would be.
I could understand your trepidation,
but what did I really do wrong?
I came to you in a panic, *yes*,
only wanting to fix our mess.
I was ill at the time, and open about that –
how I wish you'd been the same with me.
But the barriers you built, because of him,
kept me out – and locked you in.

again … and forever

i know you say *never*
but if you gave me
just *one* afternoon
and took a walk with me
you would see who i really am …

the man you fell in love with

and we could be together,
again … and *forever*

ruined

You are now gone
but the ruins remain,
sandstone reminders
of where we used to play.
Sunny days and bitter nights,
we were living
the most beautiful of lives.
But the past is past
and it's not the same,
visiting these artefacts alone …
I only have myself to blame.

beached

I sit on a wall, on the busy promenade,
watching the blue waves wash,
crashing back and forth
– turning white –
against the fringe of the land.

It's a stifling Sunday … for a change,
beads of sweat gather on my brow,
before tumbling down
– stinging my lips –
salt searing my tongue.

A smitten couple strolls,
hand in hand,
across the littered sand,
– licking ice creams –
swapping cool milky kisses.

Balls and sticks are hurled,
but quickly carried
by boisterous dogs
– sprinting headlong –
back to their families.

But I am here alone,
seeing yet unseen,
praying for someone
– for her –
to walk with me again.

your thighs

I think of you too many times.
With eyes closed, you are still a sight.
It's time to cut those reins
– be gone to the light.

… but your thighs, freckled, slight,
smooth as summer nights,
cannot easily be forced from my mind
– the memory will always linger.

… you are the crick in my neck,
the trapped nerve in my spine,
keeping me awake at night …
a pain so nice

… as nice as your thighs.

~~not~~ the one

you said that i was:
the love of your life

… but that was just a lie

you gave up on me,
in my time of need
saying that you:
just want to feel free

but only a few months on,
you are no longer alone –
already in the arms
of another special one

kaleidoscope: part two

Hints of her only. Parts of her face, glinting out from the background. Her unmistakable eyes. The mystic marble stare of green-brown that she possessed – one of the features I loved about her the most – peering from behind the camouflage of colour. *How I missed looking into those eyes.* Her smile appeared. Those gallant lips – sporting her trademark coating of rouge – opened up, curving into a smile, revealing a set of glowing white jewels. Teeth so perfectly straight and pearlescent – the whirligig colours reflecting off them, bringing more luminescence to the scene. Her nose – piercing and all. The little mole on the apple of her right cheek. Her raven hair and the linear fringe that sleeked across her brow. All the things I miss.

arrows

Breathing in,
hot deep breaths,
pulsating heartbeats
burn your chest.
Weeping eyes,
tender breasts,
compounded by
endless loneliness.
Forgotten love,
broken arrows.
Substance abuse,
no straight and narrow.

pills, pills, pills

Pills … prescribed for all the right reasons:
to relieve my physical pain, help me sleep once again.

But I started using them, abusing them
in all the wrong ways … predictably enough.

My addictive personality took over,
and now I cannot function without my pills.

It's supposed to be every four hours,
… although I rarely wait that long.

Excitement as I break the foil sleeve,
two more white tablets and all my worries drop away.

I think I have a problem – actually, I'm sure that I do,
but right now, pills are the only thing to pull me through.

They make me feel even, in a world that's at odds –
an empty life without her, passing in a marshmallow haze.

self-medicating

Self-medicating almost every night,
otherwise I would *never* sleep.

And if I'm lucky, I won't dream …
of you.

Because when I do,
it makes waking up
an unbearable thing to do.

Once again, to be without you.

every day it hurts

Every day
there is this heartache,
and every day
it grows and grows.
Every day
I think about her,
and every day
I wish it would stop.
Every day
makes me feel a little worse,
and every day
it hurts, hurts, hurts.

gambling

i go to the casino
with my mum and dad –
where i drink 'til i'm drunk,
and until i've lost …
every *thing* that i have

all the flashing lights
and the raking and spinning
are a welcome distraction –
obscuring thoughts of you …
like a passing cloud

then i recall,
the time you came with us,
and the great fun we had –
and i swear, i would lose any amount …
to gamble on love with you again

codeine

Crunching my codeine caplets,
I wash them down with watery gulps.

The opioid works its fuzzy magic –
my injured heart is slowly numbed.

My brain is fogged, my eyesight clouded:
I feel happily detached, life subdued.

The pills desensitise my entire being,
helping *me* forget what *we* went through.

Day after day of medicated bliss …
I *cannot* keep existing like this.

But … for now …
while the memories of her remain,
I will continue trying to dull my pain.

in the dark

my daylight hours are spent
in a blurred state between
prescription pills
and fantasy ...

tormenting flashbacks
of you and me

i long for night to arrive

because in the dark
is where i belong

analysis

My free days are the worst.

With nothing to occupy my hands and head,
I end up *dissecting* every mistake I made.

Analysing each *wrong* word that I said –
substituting what it should have been instead.

I take some tablets and hope to sleep –
allowing the hours of the day to *waste* away.

But even in my dreams, I still re-enact those scenes
where I wish I'd behaved differently – *better*.

my poisoning

I take my cocktail of pills,
every day, without fail.

Beta blockers and antidepressants,
painkillers – so that I cannot feel.

Putting a slew of chemicals into my body –
too many to even make me well.

But I gave up on things long ago –
and my life no longer feels my own.

I stumble through the hours
in a morose, dejected haze.

But I know exactly what I'm doing,
increasing my prescription willingly.

Unless I am with you –
I will never be happy.

And I will continue with my poisoning,
until I fail to awaken one morning.

Because there's no point in going on –
when I've let the greatest love go wrong.

shelter

thunder growls –
with a bottomless hunger:
a baritone rumble
which i can feel in my feet

lightning cracks –
with its electrostatic limbs,
galvanic blue flashes,
illuminating my room

i can see you now
hiding under the covers
and all i long to do
is shelter there with you

pluviophile

I stand at the window,
watching the rain lash down,
mourning my heartache
in a pathetic clichéd scene.

The loud tapping sound
as the drops pound the ground
acts like white noise,
soothing my overwrought mind.

Opening the window,
I stick my head outside,
inhaling the petrichor –
I can breathe easily once more.

A deep puddle pools
on the sleek-soaked tarmac,
and in the shimmering water
her glistening face appears.

A storm of emotions
swirls through my body,
joyous tears trickle down my cheeks –
she is all I can see.

Dare I hope that every time it rains
I'll get to be with her again?

obsidian

each moment away from you
transforms me into something new

i can feel my heart decaying

each ventricle and valve
artery and atrium
calcifying, turning old
spluttering to their inevitable halt

vibrant red to dusty pink
ashen grey to tragic black
the solid, marbled sculpture
that is now my obsidian heart

each moment away from you
is something i cannot get used to

lava

you are my blood –
burning, boiling,
coursing through me –
slowly, scalding,
scorching my delicate veins

a trail is left behind:
of ash, dirt and dust –
my body is molten –
without you,
it becomes an igneous rock

fault line

it's a hot summer's day

in the park with my friends,
walking on the spongy green grass –
i am smiling and laughing,
my mind almost clear – at long last

people are playing tennis
on the gravelled courts,
while children howl and laugh,
swinging and sliding in the playground

excited shouts and barking all around us –
we can barely hear each other speak –
and then a voice breaks through and shatters me –
it's another crack in my broken heart

she is there, walking her dog

my knees buckle, i struggle to stand,
shock stealing all the breath from me,
but i try to stay strong, for the sake of my friends –
this day was supposed to be about me and them

i just about manage to lift my head –
to see her – *stunning* – in *that* polka-dot dress
i mime some words, unable to talk,
and as fast as i can, continue to walk

she is soon out of sight, too far away for me to hear,
and i pretend that everything's fine –
but i know right away that it's not okay,
she has ruined my day … in the most beautiful way

polka-dot dress

i used to be whole – and a huge part of you

you let me go and my body broke,
into jagged shards of rubble and rock

time goes by slowly and i crumble further,
turning to stones and pebbles – weathered debris

now a mound of dust – the wind comes and carries me
in your direction – that's where i land

i am an unwanted speck … on your polka-dot dress
seen by you, and simply brushed away

missed milestones

I thought I'd reach all those markers –
the watershed moments supposed to make a life complete.

From a boy to a man –
no more one-night stands.
Find a proper partner, fall in love,
make her my fiancée, later my wife.

We'd turn from renters to owners –
upgrade from a flat to a house.
One child, two ... maybe even three –
a dog or a cat, to complete the family.

But things haven't turned out the way I'd like –
too late now for me to log those milestones.

My existence is quickly passing me by,
my body stiffening, hair turning grey,
becoming more and more lonely
with each turgid, empty day.

you make me sick

headaches, blurred eyes:
without you,
i don't feel right

my stomach spasms, cramps,
i double over,
collapse to the floor

in the foetal position,
i shiver and squirm,
soaked in a feverish sweat

this is it

the nausea is about to peak –
this is the sickest i have ever been
all because you are no longer near

this is how i feel –
when i think about you,
which is every day, without fail

i am not a well man

(going), (going), gone

i'm just so tired of it all –
the years and years of struggle

love and happiness finally came –
but soon they're gone and i'm alone again

i just want to be free –
no depression, panic or anxiety

to live a tranquil life –
have a family: two kids and a loving wife

maybe it'll never be that way –
and no one or *nothing* can save me

my fate, my *ending*, feels inevitable –
but i pray that *you* will try and stop it all …

before i am permanently …

                    (going)
                              (going)
                                        gone

the verge

i feel like i'm always on the verge –
that one day it'll happen
and i'll take my own life

there's a switch in my brain
that will eventually be flicked –
my being only a memory then

when she was with me, by my side,
she brought a cascade of light,
making me want to live and fight

she made me want to lead a happy life

escarpment

i see you standing at the lip of the cliff –
peering down at me from over the edge

i am at the bottom – my lowest ebb –
as i contemplate my climb to you

with my heart in my mouth, i start the ascent,
scrambling up as fast as i can –

i want you so much – that my fingers bleed,
staining the ancient, eroded rock

each nail tears off, every tendon burns,
but you are at the end of it all

i am near the top – can see your face –
as my weary legs are about to give way

i reach out with my shattered hand,
hoping that you will reach out too

instead, you say some forbidding words –
that hang in the yawning air between us

every heartbreaking syllable a slow-motion blow,
my eyes and nose cascading, in full flow

you back away from the escarpment,
out of view and out of my life

i realise there is nothing left for me …
so i release my grip, and set myself free

hippocampus

as my depression deepens
my hippocampus shrinks –
each miserable passing minute
fades another memory of you

i cling on, desperately –
to the fragments that remain,
only just recalling –
the colour of your eyes

after every failure
you drift further and further away –
i try to stay sane and happy –
for one enduring reason:

to remember your face

perpetual loss

the deep, purple-black bags
underneath my eyes,
seem to weigh down my head –
my body only just managing
to drag the rest of me around

i think of you far too much
i cannot sleep but cannot wake
i overanalyse my every mistake

my life is spent in perpetual sadness,
revisiting the pain of losing you –
and i fear i'll never be able to love again
as one more wound to my heart
would be too much for it to take

snapshots

When we take our last breaths – knowing that the end is seconds away – it will seem as if our entire existence is condensed into a series of snapshots.

Scenes from the past will skim by as we remember those we've loved and lost.

Times of absolute joy will flash before our dying eyes; wasp stings of regret feel just as sharp.

I know that when I die, I will see you, smiling, mouthing three words to me, against a backdrop of iridescent light.

Before everything turns black.

we vocal pugilists

Round after punishing round,
we trade devastating blows.
Verbal punches:
lingual uppercuts, articulated jabs.

We refuse to go down,
intent on defending ourselves,
but the ravaging bout continues
until we are both bloodied and bruised.

The final few strikes
are even more fierce, more bone-jarring,
pulverising our good memories ...
until they're no longer there.

We have both lost.

pieces

We are not just cracked;
we are completely broken.
There is not just a gap between us
but a crevasse.
Our silence is the most terrifying thing –
the absence of closeness.
How did that happen?
I know we aren't as we were,
that now we are who we need to be.
But once ... once it was just
you and me.

mythology

part man, part beast
this is what became of me …

i am now a character
in the tales that you tell –
like a figure from ancient myth
derided by your family and friends

but i am not a creature –
not an allegorical fiend –
i am a living, sentient being …
guilty only of loving a little too much

spiders

a nest is forming
in the pit of my belly

the best place for it –
this dark, secluded space

eggs hatch suddenly
insects crawling free

my stomach fills with spiders –
the sickness roils in me

it takes a while before they leave
from my mouth, my nose, my ears

leaving behind a silken trail –
intricate webs of my regret

this arachnid feeling repeats itself
each time i recall what i've lost

damaged

Take out my heart
for it has been damaged
far too often.
Diseased and dormant,
it is beyond regeneration.
Just to leave it as it is,
battered and mangled,
would be worse
than a swift, merciful release.
My poor worn-out heart:
it has been cursed.

confetti

i have finally conceded …

i destroy the last evidence of *us*
– the photographs that we got developed
– the matching ones that filled our frames
– the ones i still looked at every day

i tear them into hundreds of pieces
and throw them up into the sky outside –
glossy confetti rains down on me
but this is nothing to celebrate

i already know i'll regret this forlorn charade
next time i desperately want to see your face

charcoal

i burned it all
every single bit
of you and me
in a metal bin

i watched us turn
into a glowing flame
and then fade out again
just like reality

blackened charcoal
is what we became
and charcoal
is what we remain

i hate myself ... and you

we are too alike –
it would never work
the things i loathe in you
are the things i hate in me
our haunting, grotesque similarity

waves

It feels like I'm finally free –
and then waves of memory
come crashing over me.

As I go about my daily life –
carrying out endless menial tasks –
your face appears suddenly.

My chest hammers and my mouth dries
– I can feel a sinking sensation –
tears pool and spill from my eyes.

My world tilts, I lose my footing,
I am the axis of so much regret.
Will these waves of loss never end?

shadow dancer

in bed, unable to drift away
i stare at the smoke-stained ceiling

she appears as a moving shadow,
dancing before my watchful gaze

i shut my eyes, she disappears
and i listen to the late-night noises:

the creaking wood, gurgling pipes
… the thud of my heart

i look again, she is still there
pirouetting through my isolation

i watch for as long as i can
knowing … i never want to sleep again

with the wind tonight

I lie in bed, late at night …
so tired – eyes slitted,
leaving only a margin of sight.

Fully closed – she arrives,
in dreams and visions
I can't bear to have.

In a fevered sweat, I leap to my feet,
intent on driving away
the memories that taunt me.

I bundle to the window
and open it wide, taking deep breaths
as I gasp for my life.

Staring out, into the darkened night,
I contemplate diving outside,
floating away with the wind tonight.

old man

it's a struggle each day
– not to see your face
– or hear your voice
– or communicate with you
in any way

and as my hair turns grey
and my body winds down –
i know more than ever
that i want to be an old man,
walking slowly with you,
holding your hand

atrophy

It is all starting up again,
I can feel the looseness in my bones.
My muscles have lost their elasticity.
There's a weakness in my legs
like I'm about to fall.

My brain vibrates inside my skull,
bubbling amongst the
cerebrospinal fluid.
Please be still for a second,
and let me think!

The skin on my face is taut –
withered and flaking away.
The dark bags under my eyes,
weigh me down so much,
I can hardly raise my head.

Inside, my guts are shrinking.
Organs, tissue and cells,
all wasting away,
letting my body be, simply,
an example of human decay.

It is now only a matter of time
before all of me, gradually, atrophies.

ethanol-free

i would use alcohol, in times of struggle –
to take the edge off,
making me feel normal for a short time

temporarily calming my anxiety –
it allowed me to be *me* for her to see –
but my borrowed confidence quickly evaporated

the mornings after always demanded payback –
pounding head, shaking legs, shivering skin –
the thought of losing her, always returning

but i'm sober now, ethanol-free –
no regrets, no embarrassment, no wasted days,
only my habitual, manageable, morose ways

raw

It is fully winter now.

I walk, with no destination in mind.
My only goals: to distract, to waste time,
to dispel my nervous energy,
to help me forget (her).

As I pound the pavement,
I breathe rapidly.
My heavy exhalations fog –
floating in front of me.

The autumnal leaves
have lost their chlorophyll.
They're all yellow, and grounded,
frozen to the tarmac.

My skating-steps quicken,
sliding across the verglas.
I lose my footing – numerous times –
but refuse to slow down.

I listen to the birds –
the brave ones who have stayed,
their scattered, random chirruping
an echo of my own fragmented thoughts.

The night, the darkness,
comes down quickly.
It's only the streetlights, the cars, the ice,
the emptiness inside me, that remain.   »

My legs become stiff –
I can't feel my toes.
Tears are shivering in my eyes –
I wipe them clear with my woollen gloves.

I've been out for a while now –
my lungs are raw,
stinging and alive.
The same way she made me feel.

I will always remember (her).

seasons

the seeds of *us* were sown in spring –
our love blooming in the summer sun

we fell away with the autumn leaves –
disappearing with the winter wind

palimpsest

I take one of those late-night baths –
the kind you always used to linger in.

Stepping gingerly into the heated water,
my flesh quickly flushes pink.

I lie back in the bubbles
and stare at the spotlights in the ceiling.

The bright halogen bulbs send their beams
directly into my retinal cells.

Eventually, I close my lids –
white outlines projected behind their screen.

A figure is formed – it's her, her, her.

I open my eyes and rub them clear –
a relief to see normally again.

But with each blink that I take,
comes a negative image of her face.

Flashes of white – a palimpsest of her –
are scorched on to my brain forevermore.

kaleidoscope: part three

Her individual features started to bind together, until her entire face was there. It stayed whole for a few seconds before disappearing. Other versions appeared in turn. Different moods. Ecstatically happy, her grin pushing her cheekbones so high they created right angles, then sad. Despondent. A look of resignation, acceptance of failure. *My failures?* Orgasmic. The intimate characteristics her face would portray when in that state of quivering bliss, which only I and a few select others had been privileged to witness. I felt honoured to see the contours of that face again, no matter what mood it reflected – happy, sad, she was a sight to see, and always beautiful to me.

emergency care

Standing there – in the observant crowd –
we listen to emotional speeches,
tears threatening to spill,
lumps lodged in our painful throats.

This hospital means more to you than to me:
not just a place for you to earn a wage,
but an establishment full of love and care,
as well as … unfortunately … loss and fear.

Soon to be demolished, it is a sobering sight:
beyond its best years, with dull rain-streaked bricks,
but it remains one of Edinburgh's landmarks –
a house of protection for all the sick kids.

Holographic windmills are held on sticks –
colours spinning slowly with the warming breeze.
A brass band plays and cheers are raised –
balloons are let go, people hug and kiss.

Everyone says their reluctant *goodbyes* –
to each other and to the place –
so much history soon to be gone,
torn down, reduced to rubble and dust.

But … it's been years since that day
and the old place still stands,
its demolition delayed, its execution stayed,
and still saving children's lives up to today.

A new home was built next to the Royal Infirmary –
all shiny and modern, ready to take up the baton.
Boxes of equipment had already left –
the relocation of patients the final step.   »

Then a bombshell arrived at the very last moment –
the move postponed, the site not ready to open.
Apparatus and implements were transferred back,
reclaiming their place in the dilapidated refuge.

You were full of anger, disappointment, resignation –
I felt very sorry for all of the staff.
That day was so hard, watching everyone let go –
and then those poignant words meant nothing at all.

Maybe there will be another ceremony –
when it is *definitely* the time.
And if I see you there, I'll make sure to wave,
our shared past a memory like the rest.

a man who is not me

i think about reaching out –
to see what your life is like now

but there are things i couldn't bear to witness –
like pictures of a man who is not me

i know it will happen one day ... obviously,
you'll want to be settled with someone else ...

but hopefully when i'm no longer around to see

transmit

It's the middle of the night,
and I am wide awake.
Lying motionless in my bed,
I am thinking of you –
imagining you sleepless too,
though I doubt that's true.

Closing my eyes tightly,
I cogitate over what I would say –
explaining how I feel, how sorry I am –
hoping the words can somehow
transmit themselves to you,
through our long-abandoned telepathy.

farewell thought

My pulse beats *too* hard –
that's what you do to my heart.

Sprawled face down in bed, on the yielding mattress,
my breast batters against its coiled springs.

My pulse staggers, slows, is about to stop –
my brain conjuring up my farewell thought.

My skin is mottled underneath the sheet –
my eyes close as I try to breathe.

This *is* the end of me …
but I am seeing what I want to see –

you

still

i loved you at the start
i loved you at the end
i love you still ...
with my absolute heart

acknowledgements

I would especially like to thank the following people: Lynn Curtis, Louise Harnby, Kati Lacey, Sara Donaldson, and Viki Ottewill. All of your hard work – and patience – cannot be underestimated. I am so grateful.

As always, I would like to express my gratitude and love to my family: my mum, dad, and brother, who always support me – and put up with me – even when I'm at my most difficult, and also to my niece, Olivia, who makes me smile when it seems impossible to do so.

A final acknowledgment goes to the (nameless) person to whom this book is dedicated, and for whom most of these pieces were written, or were about. I am so sorry for my failings, and I wish I could have been better for you. I miss you. Take care.

www.ryansamturner.com

www.ingramcontent.com/pod-product-compliance
Lightning Source LLC
Chambersburg PA
CBHW020546030426
42337CB00013B/986